Hill Campus of Arts & Sciences
451 Clermont St.
Denver, CO 80220

# MOTHMAN

## THE UNSOLVED MYSTERY

BY LISA WADE McCORMICK

**Reading Consultant:**
Barbara J. Fox
Reading Specialist
North Carolina State University

**Content Consultant:**
Andrew Nichols, PhD
Executive Director
American Institute of Parapsychology
Gainesville, Florida

Capstone
press

Mankato, Minnesota

Blazers is published by Capstone Press,
151 Good Counsel Drive, P.O. Box 669, Mankato, Minnesota 56002.
www.capstonepress.com

Books published by Capstone Press are manufactured with paper
containing at least 10 percent post-consumer waste.

*Library of Congress Cataloging-in-Publication Data*
McCormick, Lisa Wade, 1961–
    Mothman: the unsolved mystery / by Lisa Wade McCormick.
    p. cm. — (Blazers. Mysteries of science)
    Summary: "Presents the legend of Mothman, including current theories and famous
encounters" — Provided by publisher.
    Includes bibliographical references (p. 31) and index.
    ISBN: 978-1-4296-3395-6 (library binding)
    1. Mothman — Juvenile literature. I. Title. II. Series.
QL89.2.M68M33 2010
001.944 — dc22                                        2009005057

**Editorial Credits**
Katy Kudela, editor; Alison Thiele, set designer; Ashlee Suker, book designer;
    Svetlana Zhurkin, media researcher

**Photo Credits**
AP Images/Jeff Gentner, 10–11, 23, 28–29
Cathy Wilkins, 20
Courtesy Jeff Wamsley, 6–7, 8; photo from *The Athens Messenger,*
    Athens, Ohio, 9
Courtesy Mark Phillips, 4–5
Fortean Picture Library, cover, 12–13, 21, 26
iStockphoto/Randy Plett, 22
Natalie "Orbyss" Grewe, 18–19
Shutterstock/Marilyn Volan, grunge background (throughout); Maugli,
    16–17 (background); rgbspace, (paper art element) 3, 17; Shmeliova
    Natalia, 16 (paper art element); Tony Campbell, 24–25; Vlade Shestakov, 27
Svetlana Zhurkin, 14–15

The author would like to thank Jeff Wamsley of the Mothman Museum in Point Pleasant,
West Virginia, and paranormal investigator Joe Nickell for their help with this book.

# TABLE OF CONTENTS

## CHAPTERS

## FEATURES

# A RED-EYED BEING

Two young couples spot something strange near an old power plant. They move closer to get a better look. The couples see a creature with large wings and glowing red eyes.

Did the North Power Plant house a monster? In the 1960s, some people said they saw a creature near the empty building.

The couples race back to their small West Virginia town. They drive more than 100 miles (161 kilometers) per hour. They hear giant wings beating as the creature follows them.

## MOTHMAN FACT

After the sightings, the two couples went back to the power plant area. They found hooflike prints in the ground.

A person who claimed to see Mothman drew the creature as half man and half bird.

7

# Couples Say They Saw 6-Ft. 100-mph 'Bird'

What did Linda Scarberry, her husband, and two friends see on November 15, 1966? Was it the famous Mothman?

Linda Scarberry (far right), her husband, and friends believe they saw Mothman.

The small town of Point Pleasant, West Virginia, became famous for its Mothman sightings.

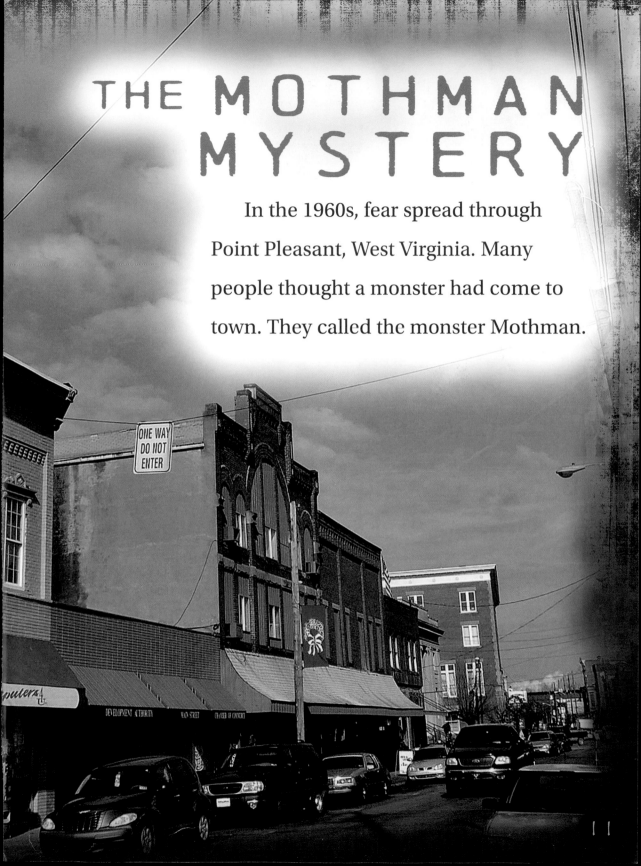

# THE MOTHMAN MYSTERY

In the 1960s, fear spread through Point Pleasant, West Virginia. Many people thought a monster had come to town. They called the monster Mothman.

ONE WAY
DO NOT
ENTER

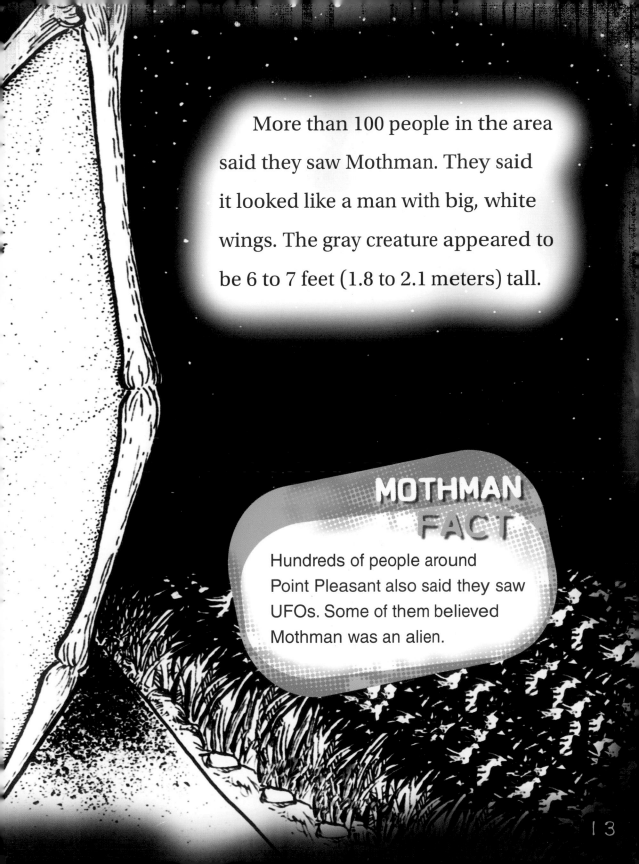

More than 100 people in the area said they saw Mothman. They said it looked like a man with big, white wings. The gray creature appeared to be 6 to 7 feet (1.8 to 2.1 meters) tall.

## MOTHMAN FACT

Hundreds of people around Point Pleasant also said they saw UFOs. Some of them believed Mothman was an alien.

The Mothman's eyes are what people remembered most. They said the creature's large, red eyes seemed to glow.

**MOTHMAN FACT**

Many people said Mothman's eyes cast a spell on them. They could not stop staring at the creature's red eyes.

# FAMOUS SIGHTINGS

 Linda Scarberry's story was not the first Mothman sighting. A few days earlier, Kenneth Duncan claimed he saw a creature near Clendenin, West Virginia. He said the strange being flew past him while he was digging a grave.

 The day before Scarberry's sighting, Newell Partridge of Salem, West Virginia, said he saw a creature with red eyes. His dog chased the being into a field. The dog never came back.

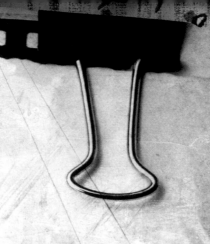

 On November 16, 1966, six people claimed a creature followed them to a house near Point Pleasant. The red-eyed being stared through a window and then flew away.

 On November 25, 1966, Tom Ury said he saw a large, gray figure near Point Pleasant. He said the creature flew over his car.

# SEARCHING FOR MOTHMAN

In 1966, police searched the woods for Mothman. They talked to witnesses. But all police found were a few odd footprints.

## MOTHMAN FACT

Stories of Mothman became famous. A movie was made telling of the strange events in Point Pleasant.

19

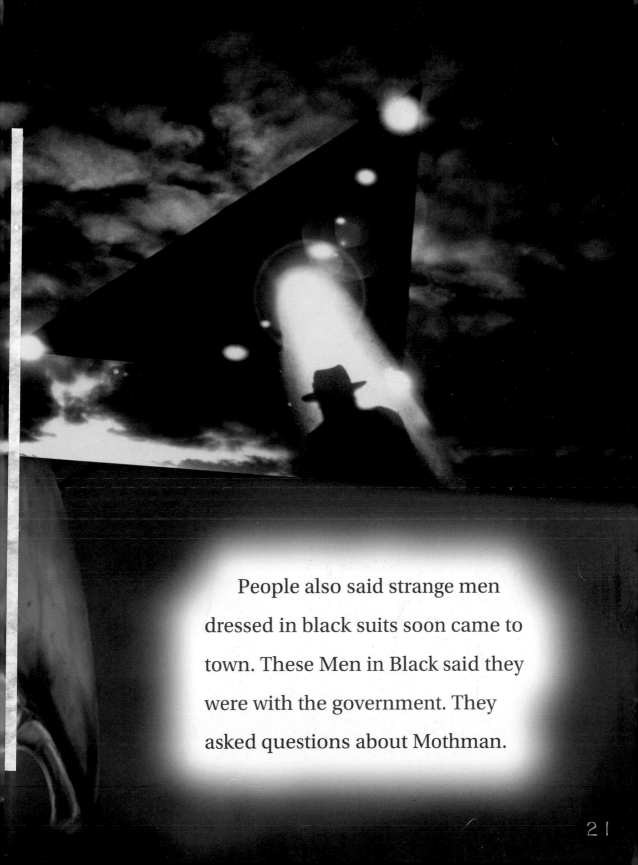

People also said strange men dressed in black suits soon came to town. These Men in Black said they were with the government. They asked questions about Mothman.

Paranormal investigators have also looked for Mothman. They wondered if Mothman was a supernatural being.

paranormal investigator — someone who studies events that science can't explain
supernatural — something that cannot be given an ordinary explanation

# MOTHMAN OR BIRD?

Some scientists believed Mothman was a bird. They said it was a barred owl or a sandhill crane.

## MOTHMAN FACT

Witnesses claimed Mothman was bigger and faster than an owl or a crane.

In 1986, people claimed they saw a strange creature near a nuclear power plant in Ukraine. The creature had large wings and red eyes.

Other people agreed Mothman was a bird. They said the bird got into chemicals at the power plant. These chemicals changed the bird into a strange creature.

There are still a few reports of Mothman today. People around the world say they have seen the creature.

What do you think? Was Mothman a bird? Or is this a **mystery** that will never be solved?

**mystery** — something that is hard to explain or understand

A speaker from the Mothman Museum in Point Pleasant shares stories.

# GLOSSARY

**alien** (AY-lee-uhn) — a creature from another planet

**mystery** (MISS-tur-ee) — something that is hard to explain or understand

**paranormal investigator** (pa-ruh-NOR-muhl in-VESS-tuh-gate-ur) — someone who studies events that science can't explain

**power plant** (POU-ur PLANT) — a building or group of buildings used to create electricity

**supernatural** (soo-pur-NACH-ur-uhl) — something that cannot be given an ordinary explanation

**UFO** (YOO EF OH) — an object in the sky thought to be a spaceship from another planet; UFO is short for Unidentified Flying Object.

**witness** (WIT-niss) — a person who has seen or heard something

# READ MORE

**Hamilton, Sue L.** *Monsters of Mystery.* Unsolved Mysteries. Edina, Minn.: ABDO, 2008.

**Herbst, Judith.** *Monsters.* The Unexplained. Minneapolis: Lerner, 2005.

**Sertori, J. M**. *Monsters.* The Unexplained. Milwaukee: Gareth Stevens, 2006.

# INTERNET SITES

FactHound offers a safe, fun way to find Internet sites related to this book. All of the sites on FactHound have been researched by our staff.

Here's all you do:

Visit *www.facthound.com*

FactHound will fetch the best sites for you!

# INDEX